MUSIC OF THE

Reader's Digest
PIANO  LIBRARY

Masters

0 MASTERPIECES FOR SOLO PIANO BY 10 GREAT COMPOSERS

Compiled and edited by Heather Ramage
Cover design by Josh Labouve
Cover photograph © Comstock Images
Master recordings supplied by kind permission of Reader's Digest Music

This book Copyright © 2008 by Amsco Publications,
A Division of Music Sales Publications, New York

Exclusive Distributors:
Music Sales Corporation
257 Park Avenue South, New York, NY 10010, USA
Music Sales Limited
14-15 Berners Street, London, W1T 3LJ, England
Music Sales Pty. Limited
20 Resolution Drive, Caringbah, NSW 2229, Australia.

Order No. AM993927
ISBN: 978.0.8256.3644.8

Printed in the United States of America by
Vicks Lithograph and Printing Corporation

D1088964

Amsco Publications
A Part of **The Music Sales Group**
New York/London/Paris/Sydney/Copenhagen/Berlin/Tokyo/Madrid

COMPACT DISC TRACK LISTING

N.B. *Please note that the musical arrangements included in this book
may not exactly match the corresponding audio.*

TABLE OF CONTENTS

N.B. *To avoid awkward page turns the running order of this book differs slightly to that on the CDs.*

ABOUT THE COMPOSERS

JOHANN SEBASTIAN BACH (1685–1750) was the greatest composer for the church in music history. No one else has come close in quantity and quality: hundreds of cantatas, passions, oratorios, chorales, settings of the Latin Mass, motets, and organ preludes. The most famous of the four Bach pieces in this collection—"Jesu Bleibet Meine Freude" ("Jesu, Joy of Man's Desiring")—is from one of his religious works, Cantata No. 147 (*Herz und Mund und Tat und Leben,* 1723). This timeless chorale is still often performed at church services and weddings.

Even if one discounted his religious works, Bach would still rank as a master composer on the basis of his keyboard works: fugues, preludes and variations, sonatas, and concertos. He also wrote cantatas on secular subjects, such as the "Hunting Cantata" (No. 208, *Was mir behagt,* 1713), which contains the well-known aria "Sheep May Safely Graze," included here. In addition, we have the opening aria of his *Goldberg Variations* (1741), which he reportedly wrote for his friend Johann Gottlieb Goldberg to play late at night for Goldberg's insomniac noble patron. The Oscar™-winning film *The English Patient* features this poignant melody. Our final Bach offering is the first movement of his Italian Concerto (BWV 971, 1735), originally written for a harpsichord with two manuals or keyboards.

LUDWIG VAN BEETHOVEN (1770–1827) deserted the classical style of Mozart and Haydn, both of whom he revered, and forged a shocking new style of *Sturm und Drang* from the ideals of Romanticism. He touched something deep in the human psyche, and his music is just as compelling and fascinating today as two centuries ago when it first appeared. Ironically, he left much of Romanticism behind late in life and went "retro"—not back to Mozart and Haydn—but to Bach, writing monumental fugues for piano, string quartet, and even orchestra. And it bears repeating that he became the world's greatest composer while deteriorating into total deafness during the last 20 years of his life.

Our first Beethoven composition included here, Piano Sonata No. 14 in C♯ Minor "Moonlight" (Op. 27, No. 2; 1800–1), is one of the most famous classical piano works ever written. The sombre, rippling open chords of the Adagio sostenuto reminded the critic Ludwig Rellstab of the moonlight reflecting on Lake Lucerne—hence its nickname. Tremendous emotion is held in check in this first movement, only to be unleashed like a tornado later in the sonata.

Everyone knows the opening motif of Beethoven's Symphony No. 5 in C Minor, and that it supposedly signifies fate or destiny. Along with the "fate" theme of the Fifth, we have in this volume the joyful theme of the last movement of Beethoven's Symphony No. 6 in F Major, the "Pastoral." It is often cited as a supreme example of program music describing a scene or event—the words "recollections of rural life" appear in Beethoven's own notes on the score.

JOHANNES BRAHMS (1833–1897) had an unusual beginning for a classical composer, cutting his teeth on old pianos in the bars and brothels of his native Hamburg, Germany. But he went on to become a favorite of classical audiences both for his own music and his conducting skills. His oeuvre includes four symphonies, several concertos, much chamber music, and many songs. He is not known as an innovator, but rather as a follower of the styles of Bach and Beethoven.

In 1869 Brahms arranged some Hungarian dances for two pianos, and the vibrant Hungarian Dance No. 5 in G Minor from that set—included here—became one of his most famous works. Of course, it would be sacrilege not to include his beloved "Lullaby," written in 1868, the same year as his German Requiem. We also have the theme from the third movement of his Symphony No. 3 in F Major and his Intermezzo in A Major Op. 118, No. 2 from *Six Piano Pieces.*

FRÉDÉRIC CHOPIN (1810–1849) made his concert debut at age eight in Warsaw, and was writing sophisticated piano works by his mid-teens. When he moved to Paris in 1830 at 20 years old he was a fully developed artist. Chopin preferred smaller forms (études, preludes, waltzes, nocturnes) for the insular world of Parisian salons, but their range of mood, rich harmonies, and subtlety made them "seem boundless," as one critic put it. He died at 39 of tuberculosis after a long love affair with novelist George Sand.

Chopin's works are at the core of the piano repertoire, and the four pieces in this volume are among his best known and loved. Chopin himself said he had never written another melody as beautiful as the Étude in E Major "Tristesse" (Op. 10, No. 3; 1833). The "Minute" Valse in D♭ Major is from his last group of waltzes (Op. 64, No. 1; 1847). Chopin's publisher created the nickname, meaning "small," while the composer originally titled it "Petit chien" (Little Dog). One of Chopin's biographers said the piece depicts a dog chasing its tail.

GEORGE FRIDERIC HANDEL (1685-1759) and Bach were the two giants of the late-Baroque era. German by birth, Handel went to Rome to study and compose Italian opera. After making London his permanent base in 1712, he wrote three dozen operas for aristocratic audiences. He also excelled at oratorios on biblical subjects, which showcased his unparalleled talent for writing for the human voice. His most famous oratorio, *Messiah* (1741), is still a fixture at Christmas throughout the Western world. This collection features its stirring and majestic "Hallelujah Chorus," as well as the chorus "See, the Conqu'ring Hero Comes" from *Judas Maccabaeus* (1746), written to celebrate the defeat of the Jacobite Rebellion. Handel composed for numerous royal occasions, for example, *Water Music* for King George I, which contains the beautiful "Air" included here. The lovely "Sarabande," also in this volume, was featured in the 1975 Stanley Kubrick film *Barry Lyndon.*

FRANZ JOSEPH HAYDN (1732–1809) is generally regarded to be among the top five classical composers after the three giants: Bach, Beethoven, and Mozart. Who the fifth might be is more subjective, with this writer's vote going to Tchaikovsky. Both Haydn and Mozart represent the epitome of the classical style: clarity, form (especially the sonata form), and lightheartedness.

Haydn spent most of his career as music director for the wealthy Esterházy family of Austria-Hungary. With a private orchestra at his disposal, he churned out more than 100 symphonies, many with musical jokes. The best-known example is his Symphony No. 94 in G Major, nicknamed "Surprise" because of the loud chord in the slow second movement, which has been included in this album.

Haydn was also the first great master of the string quartet, with about 80 to his credit. Representing his output in that genre is the beautiful Andante cantabile from String Quartet No. 17 in F Major "Serenade" (Op. 3, No. 5), heard in the film *Bread and Chocolate*. Also featured in this collection are two Haydn piano works: Adagio in F Major (Hob. XVII) and Piano Sonata No. 4 in G Major (Third Movement: Presto).

WOLFGANG AMADEUS MOZART (1756–1791) almost defies description. A child prodigy who dazzled European nobility, he wrote more than 600 compositions: 41 symphonies, 27 piano concertos, 18 operas, 17 masses, and 24 string quartets, to name but a portion of his massive output. He was only 35 when he died of typhus in Vienna. One can't help imagine what musical wonders he would have created had he lived as long as Beethoven or Haydn.

Mozart's works are still central to the classical canon, and most composers who came after were influenced by him. One such grateful composer was Tchaikovsky, who in his *Mozartiana Suite* orchestrated three of Mozart's piano works, as well as the motet "Ave Verum Corpus."

Included in this collection are his celebrated "Allelujah" from the motet *Exsultate, Jubilate* (K. 165), which Mozart wrote for castrato voice with orchestra. We also have the "Rondo Alla Turca" ("Turkish Rondo"), familiar to most piano students, and the finale of his Piano Sonata No. 11 in A Major (K. 331). The Symphony No. 40 in G Minor (K. 550) is the most performed of Mozart's symphonies. The agitated melody of the first movement (Molto allegro) gives way to one of his grandest themes.

PYOTR ILYICH TCHAIKOVSKY (1840–1893), emotionally sensitive ever since his youth, had a supreme gift for rapturous melodies that explore the nuances of tragic love. The work that best exemplifies his "impassioned lyricism" (as one critic called it) is his Piano Concerto No. 1 in B♭ Minor, which his mentor Nikolay Rubinstein initially deemed unplayable. His symphonies are among the greatest ever written, especially Symphony No. 5 in E Minor and Symphony No. 6 in B Minor ("Pathétique").

Tchaikovsky died nine days after the premiere of the Sixth symphony in 1893. The most-cited cause is cholera from unboiled water, but some prefer the romantic rumor that he committed suicide rather than face the scandal of a homosexual affair.

Tchaikovsky's ballets contain unforgettable melodies, as evidenced here by "Dance of the Cygnets" from *Swan Lake*. The first performance of that ballet in 1877 was a disaster, and it had to wait until 1895 in a production by Marius Petipa to achieve its rightful acclaim. The song "None But the Lonely Heart," also included, is from a group of songs (Op. 6) written soon after his famous *Romeo and Juliet Fantasy Overture* in 1869.

ANTONIO VIVALDI (1678–1741), known as the "Red Priest" for the color of his hair, was born and lived mostly in Venice. He taught violin and composed for the Ospedale della Pietà, an institution for orphaned girls, where the nobility congregated for musical performances. Vivaldi wrote nearly 500 concertos in the Baroque style for violin, mandolin, guitar, and other instruments. Three of his concertos are in this volume: the third movement of "Autumn" from *The Four Seasons*, the first movement of Concerto for Two Mandolins, Strings and Organ in G Major, and the first movement of Concerto No. 8 for Two Violins in A Minor from *L'estro armonico*. Vivaldi also composed notable sacred works, represented here by the opening Largo from *Stabat Mater*. He was one of the first composers to benefit financially from publishing his music. After his death, he was virtually forgotten until the second half of the 20th century, which saw a major revival of his works.

RICHARD WAGNER (1813–1883) wrote 14 operas, both music and words, and it is on those his reputation rests. He was a larger-than-life figure, seducing two wives of men close to him. The first, Mathilde, spouse of his patron Wesendonck, and the second, Cosima, wife of conductor Hans von Bülow and daughter of Franz Liszt. After divorcing von Bülow, Cosima married Wagner and they had three children. His operas— products of an out-sized personality—are on a huge scale, much longer than typical operas, more symphonically based, and contain mystical plots from German legend. Wagner's goal was a new kind of music drama that fused together all elements of the arts, and he built his own theater at Bayreuth, Bavaria to stage them. His music tends to elicit extreme reactions— either you love him or hate him.

Three of the Wagner selections in this collection are from his opera *Tannhäuser* (1845), about a minstrel torn between erotic and chaste love. The final selection is his "Ride of the Valkyries" from *Die Walküre*, featured as the hair-raising background music to the unforgettable helicopter scene in the 1979 film *Apocalypse Now*.

By Rick Hessney

Aria
from *Goldberg Variations*
Composed by Johann Sebastian Bach

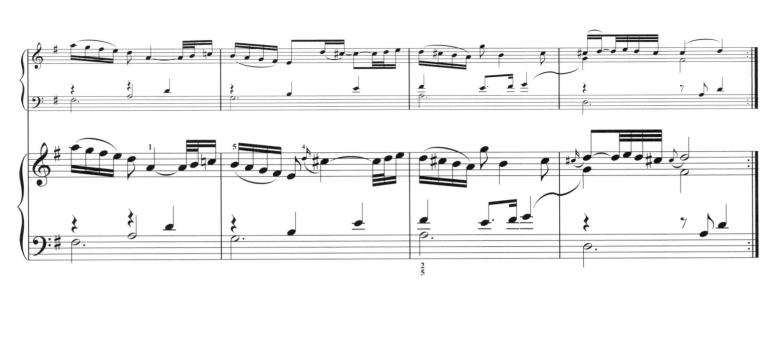

Italian Concerto
1st Movement: Allegro
Composed by Johann Sebastian Bach

Jesu, Joy of Man's Desiring

from *Cantata 147*

Composed by Johann Sebastian Bach

rall. poco a poco

Sheep May Safely Graze
from *Cantata 208*

Composed by Johann Sebastian Bach

D.C. al Coda ⊕

⊕ Coda

rall.

f

p

Turkish March
from *The Ruins of Athens*

Composed by Ludwig van Beethoven

Piano Sonata No. 14 in C♯ Minor

Op. 27, No. 2 "Moonlight"

1st Movement: Adagio sostenuto

Composed by Ludwig van Beethoven

28

Symphony No. 5 in C Minor

1st Movement: Theme

Composed by Ludwig van Beethoven

32

Symphony No. 6 in F Major
"Pastoral"
5th Movement: Allegretto theme

Composed by Ludwig van Beethoven

35

Hungarian Dance No. 5 in G Minor

Composed by Johannes Brahms

Intermezzo in A Major
Op. 118, No. 2
from *Six Piano Pieces*
Composed by Johannes Brahms

Andante teneramente

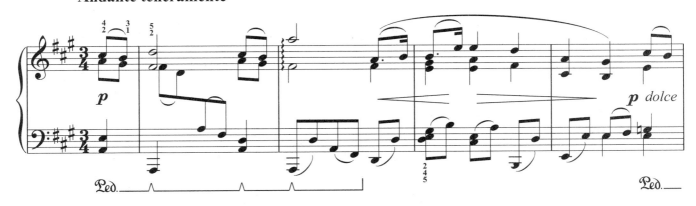

43

Lullaby
Op. 49, No. 4

Composed by Johannes Brahms

47

Symphony No. 3 in F Major
3rd Movement: Poco allegretto

Composed by Johannes Brahms

49

poco rit.

Étude in E Major

Op. 10, No. 3 "Tristesse"

Composed by Frédéric Chopin

N.B. This piece is a simplified arrangement of the original

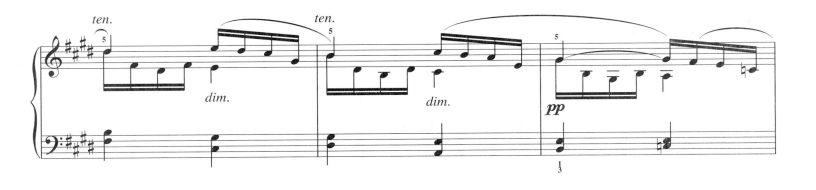

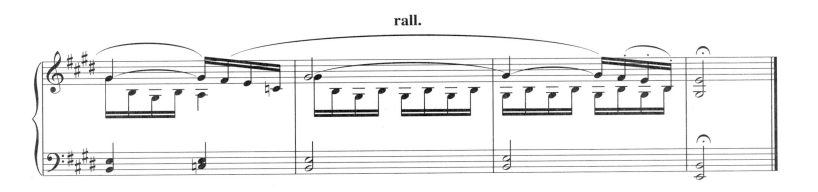

Mazurka in B♭ Major
Op. 7, No. 1

Composed by Frédéric Chopin

Ped. simile

p legato

Ped._____ Ped._____ Ped._____ Ped._____

poco rall.　　a tempo

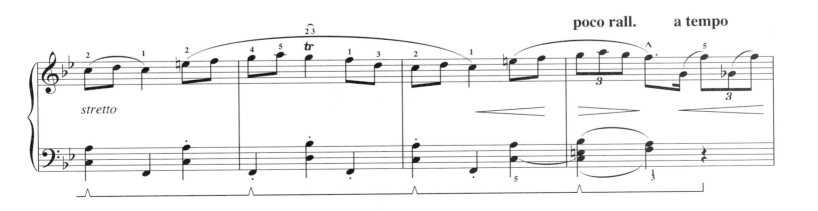

stretto

Nocturne in E♭ Major

Op. 9, No. 2

Composed by Frédéric Chopin

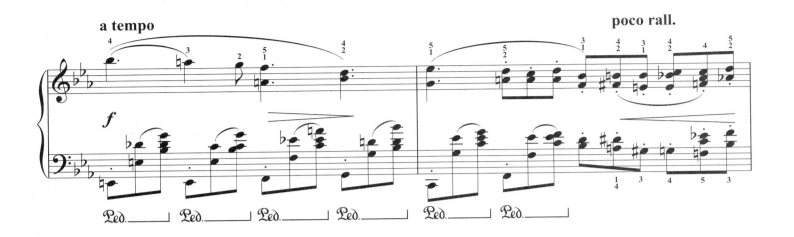

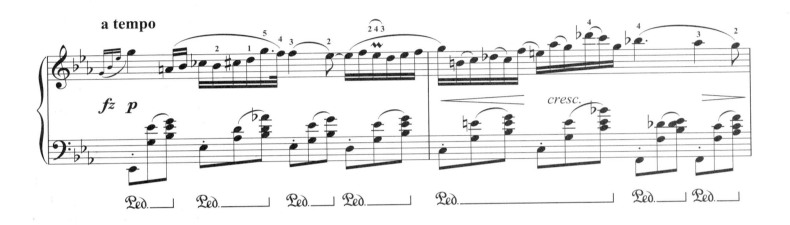

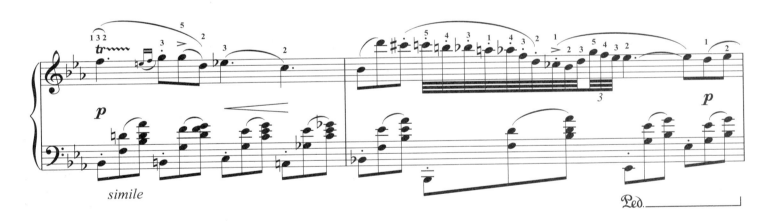

poco rall.   a tempo

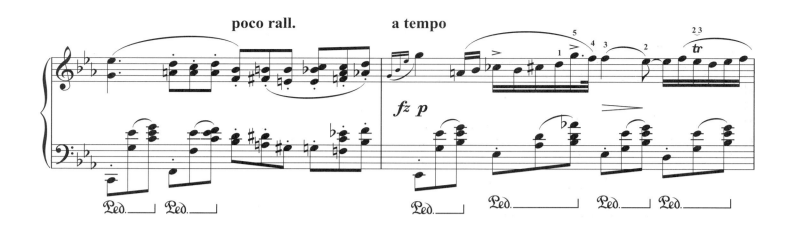

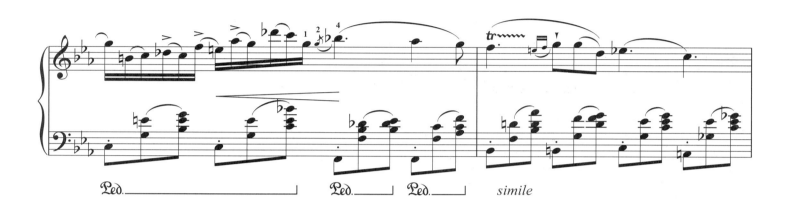

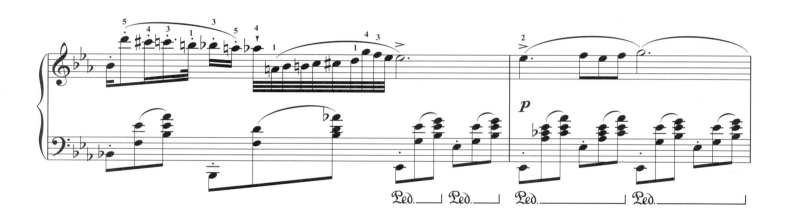

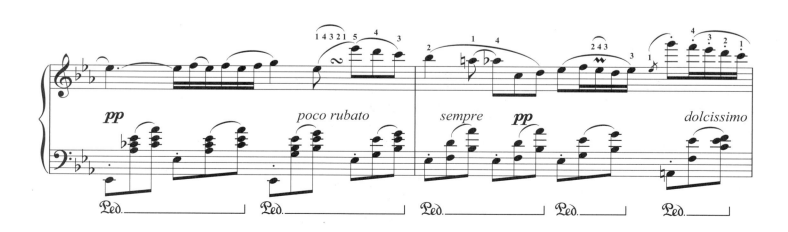

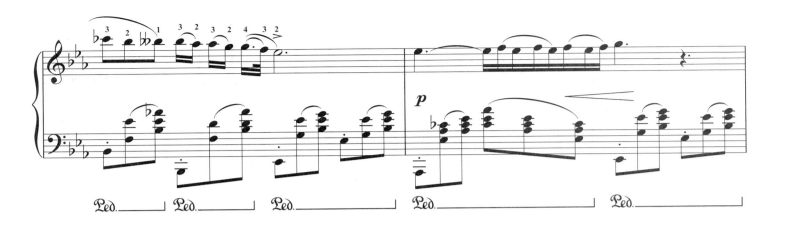

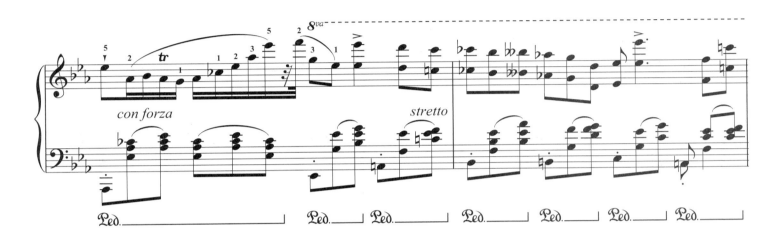

Valse in D♭ Major
Op. 64, No. 1 "Minute"

Composed by Frédéric Chopin

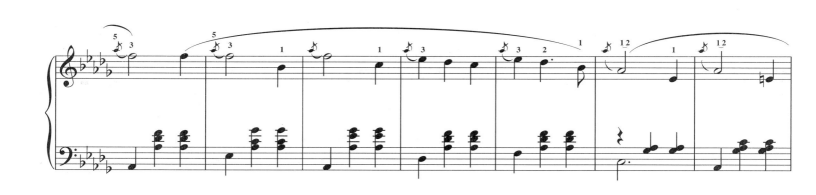

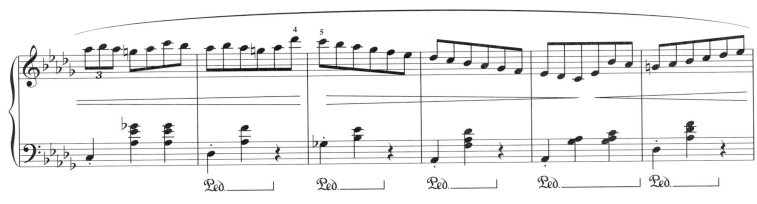

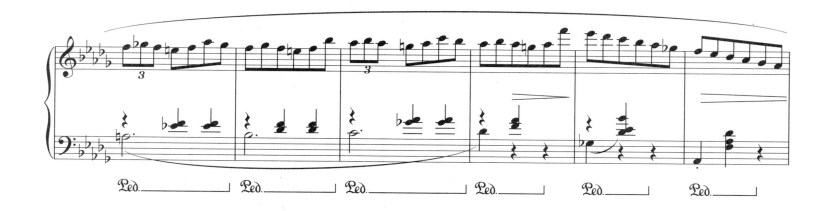

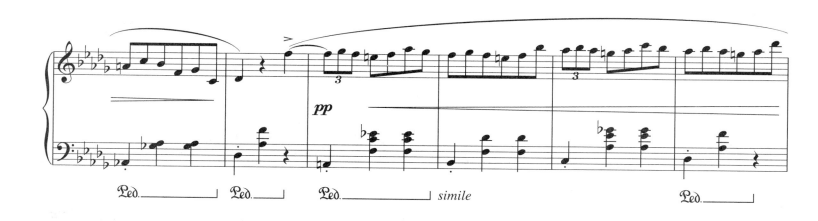

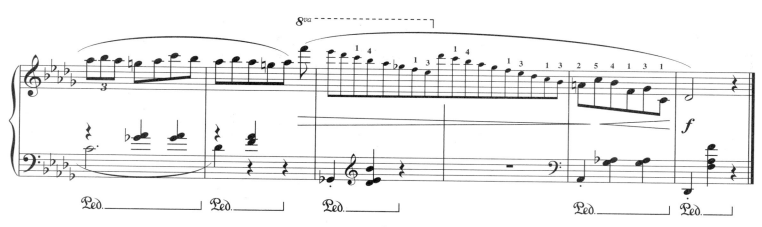

Air
from *Water Music*

Composed by George Frideric Handel

Hallelujah Chorus
from *Messiah*

Composed by George Frideric Handel

Allegro (♩ = 104)

mf *sempre marcato*

See, the Conqu'ring Hero Comes

from *Judas Maccabaeus*

Composed by George Frideric Handel

Sarabande
from *Harpsichord Suite in D Minor*

Composed by George Frideric Handel

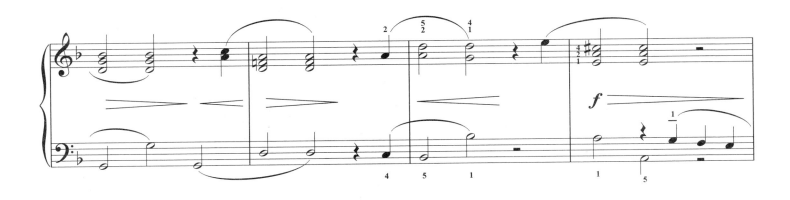

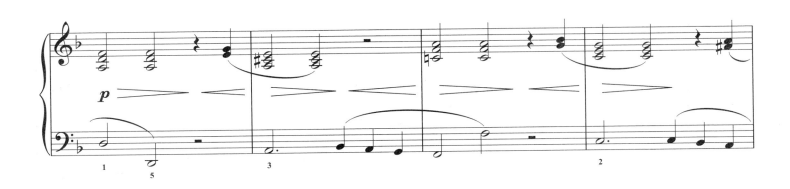

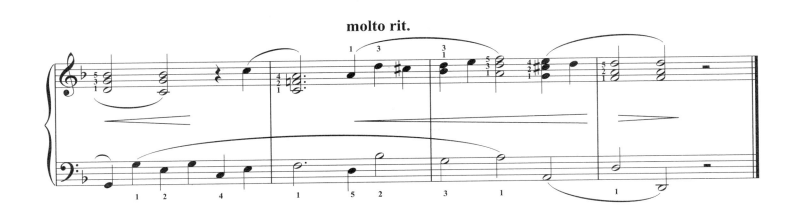

81

Adagio in F Major
Hob. XVII

Composed by Franz Joseph Haydn

ring Quartet No. 17 in F Major
Op. 3, No. 5 "Serenade"
2nd Movement: Andante cantabile

Composed by Franz Joseph Haydn

85

Piano Sonata No. 4 in G Major
3rd Movement: Presto
Composed by Franz Joseph Haydn

Symphony No. 94 in G Major

"Surprise"
2nd Movement: Theme

Composed by Franz Joseph Haydn

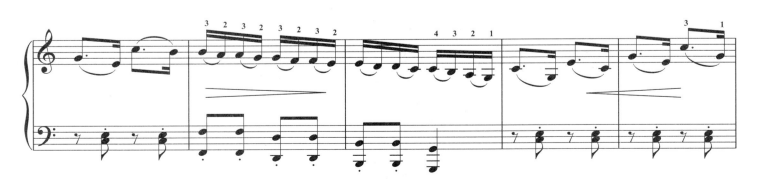

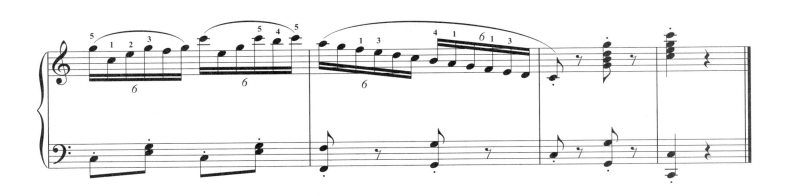

Allelujah
from *Exsultate, Jubilate*

Composed by Wolfgang Amadeus Mozart

Minuet in D

K. 355

Composed by Wolfgang Amadeus Mozart

Piano Sonata No. 11 in A Major
3rd Movement: Rondo Alla Turca

Composed by Wolfgang Amadeus Mozart

Symphony No. 40 in G Minor
1st Movement: Molto allegro

Composed by Wolfgang Amadeus Mozart

None But the Lonely Heart

Op. 6, No. 6

from *Six Songs*

Composed by Pyotr Ilyich Tchaikovsky

Dance of the Cygnets
from *Swan Lake*

Composed by Pyotr Ilyich Tchaikovsky

Serenade for Strings in C Major
Op. 48
2nd Movement: Waltz

Composed by Pyotr Ilyich Tchaikovsky

A Winter Morning
Op. 39, No. 2
from *Album for the Young*

Composed by Pyotr Ilyich Tchaikovsky

Grand March
from *Tannhäuser*

Composed by Richard Wagner

Maestro (Overture)

117

Pilgrim's Chorus
from *Tannhäuser*

Composed by Richard Wagner

To the Evening Star
from *Tannhäuser*

Composed by Richard Wagner

Ride of the Valkyries

from *Die Walküre*

Composed by Richard Wagner

Autumn
from *The Four Seasons*
3rd Movement: Allegro

Composed by Antonio Vivaldi

Concerto for Two Mandolins, Strings and Organ in G Major

1st Movement: Allegro

Composed by Antonio Vivaldi

Concerto No. 8 for Two Violins in A Minor

from *L'estro armonico*

1st Movement: Allegro

Composed by Antonio Vivaldi

Stabat Mater
from *Stabat Mater*

Composed by Antonio Vivaldi